EXTRATERRESTRIAL LIFE

Aliens in Pop Culture

Hal Marcovitz

ReferencePoint Press®

San Diego, CA

© 2012 ReferencePoint Press, Inc.
Printed in the United States

For more information, contact:
ReferencePoint Press, Inc.
PO Box 27779
San Diego, CA 92198
www. ReferencePointPress.com

LIBRARY OF CONGRESS CATALOGING-IN-PUBLICATION DATA

Marcovitz, Hal.
  Aliens in pop culture / by Hal Marcovitz.
    p. cm. -- (Extraterrestrial life series)
  Includes bibliographical references and index.
  ISBN-13: 978-1-60152-154-5 (hardback)
  ISBN-10: 1-60152-154-5 (hardback)
  1. Extraterrestrial beings in popular culture--Juvenile literature. I. Title.
  CB156.M36 2011
  001.942--dc22
                                                                2010045683

CONTENTS

The Enduring Popularity of Extraterrestrials

The opening words of the 1898 novel *The War of the Worlds* warn readers they are in for a frightening experience. "Across the gulf of space," wrote British author H.G. Wells, "minds that are to our minds as ours are to those of the beasts that perish, intellects vast and cool and unsympathetic, regarded this Earth with envious eyes, and slowly drew their plans against us."[1]

As readers soon discover, it does not take long for bad things to happen to the people of Earth. The Martian invaders land and quickly build machines of destruction, which they use to obliterate the cities of Earth. The Martians are evil and relentless, using a heat ray to incinerate tens of millions of people. Just when things look bleakest, though, humankind prevails and the invaders are defeated. Near the conclusion of the story, the author wrote, "We have learned now that

> **DID YOU KNOW?**
>
> In the novel *The War of the Worlds*, the first Martian ship lands near London, England. For the 1938 radio adaptation, the producers rewrote the story so that the first ship landed near Grover's Mill, New Jersey.

we cannot regard this planet as being fenced in and a secure hiding place for Man; we can never anticipate the unseen good or evil that may come upon us suddenly out of space."[2]

More than a century after its publication, *The War of the Worlds* remains one of the most popular stories in the history of science-fiction literature. The book has never been out of print—the most recent edition was published in 2010. Over the years, the story has been adapted into many TV and film versions. A 1953 film version was selected by a panel of more than 50 scientists as one of the top 10 science-fiction films of all time. A half century later, a film adaptation starring Tom Cruise and Dakota Fanning

The alien invasion from Mars, as envisioned by author H.G. Wells, targets London, England, as alien spacecraft point their death rays at the Houses of Parliament and ships on the River Thames. Wells's War of the Worlds *is one of the most popular science-fiction stories.*

racked up international box-office sales of more than $600 million. Says science-fiction historian John Clute, "H.G. Wells's 1898 novel, *The War of the Worlds*, was the first science fiction novel to make aliens seem plausible, and to give them a reasonable motive for leaving the planet: they needed the green fields of Earth, and will wipe us out to get them."[3]

"Are We Alone?"

The enduring popularity of *The War of the Worlds* illustrates how stories about extraterrestrial life have come to dominate American popular culture. In the decades since Wells wrote his novel of alien invasion, extraterrestrials and unidentified flying objects, or UFOs, have not only found a home in literature but in other forms of popular culture as well: movies, TV shows, comic books, graphic novels, and video games. Even advertisements have featured visitors from outer space. One recent advertising campaign found aliens flying all the way to Earth in pursuit of Hostess chocolate snack cakes. "To make it entertaining and stand out, it's nice to have aliens,"[4] says advertising executive Dion Hughes.

Although extraterrestrials might make very good twenty-first-century salespeople for snack cakes and other consumer products, their appeal goes back well before anybody advertised to sell anything—even before Wells published his landmark novel. Physicist Sidney Perkowitz suggests that people may have wondered about aliens from the earliest years of human civilization. He says:

> Probably since humans first saw the stars in the night sky, we have wondered about the universe. What's out there? How and when did it begin? How big is it? Will it end, and when? What's our place and purpose in it, if any? And knowing that we live in a huge cosmos with cold, empty spaces between the stars, always there is one last question: Are we alone?[5]

Panic in the Streets

Over the decades, as authors, filmmakers, video game designers, and other creative people continually conjured up new stories about aliens, scientists have insisted that there is no evidence of intelligent life anywhere except on Earth. Says astronomer Seth Shostak, "There isn't any evidence of extraterrestrial life, compelling evidence. In fact, the bottom line is . . . we haven't found extraterrestrials."[6]

While most Americans would probably agree with Shostak, a very significant minority disagrees. A 2005 poll by the Gallup organization reported that 24 percent of Americans believe extraterrestrials have visited Earth. Years ago a lot of people turned into believers thanks to one of the most bizarre adaptations of *The War of the Worlds* that has ever been produced. On the night of October 30, 1938, a national radio broadcast of the story sparked panic in many cities as thousands of listeners truly believed what they heard: that Martians had landed and launched an invasion of America.

Many people fled their homes. In cities telephone lines were flooded by callers seeking to contact loved ones. Police stations were besieged by frightened citizens. Many people ran aimlessly through the streets, too terrified to know what to do next. Said New Yorker Samuel Tishman:

> **DID YOU KNOW?**
>
> Scientists told researchers at the Gallup organization that few women believe in alien visitors because studies show many girls lose interest in science at age 12.

I came home at 9:15 P.M. just in time to receive a telephone call from my nephew who was frantic with fear. He told me the city was about to be bombed from the air and advised me to get out of the building at once. I turned on the radio and heard the broadcast which corroborated what my nephew had said, grabbed my hat and coat and a few personal belongings and ran to the elevator. When I got to the street there were hundreds of people milling around in panic. I ran out in the street with scores of others, and found people running in all directions.[7]

Today, in an era of high-definition TV, state-of-the-art computer graphics, and films shot in 3-D, it is hard to imagine a radio drama sparking widespread panic, but in the 1930s radio was a popular and compelling medium of communication. Each day, millions of people turned on their radios to listen to news, music, and other entertainment. In that respect, the panic that gripped many people who heard the broadcast is understandable. Best-selling horror novelist Stephen King points out that radio may have been the perfect medium at the time for an adaptation of *The War of the Worlds*. Back then, he says, the special effects available to filmmakers were still quite rudimentary. If a movie had been made of *The War of the Worlds*, King says, it would not have sparked a panic by audience members, who could probably have plainly seen the zippers running down the backs of the costumes of the Martians. "Radio made it real,"[8] King says.

Back in 1938 few people would probably have believed that stories about alien invaders would eventually come to dominate popular culture. But on the night before Halloween, *The War of the Worlds* helped convince a lot of people that the aliens had arrived—and were here to stay.

CHAPTER ONE

The Aliens Arrive

By the time H.G. Wells published *The War of the Worlds*, science fiction had already become a popular genre among readers. Nearly a century before Wells wrote his tale of alien invasion, a young Englishwoman, Mary Shelley, concocted a frightening tale about a scientist who creates life in the laboratory by stitching together the parts of bodies he exhumes from graves. She named her story *Frankenstein*.

In the mid-1800s, French author Jules Verne wrote a number of science-fiction classics, including *Journey to the Centre of the Earth*, which tells the story of travelers who uncover a hidden civilization miles beneath the surface of the planet. Verne also authored *Twenty Thousand Leagues Under the Sea*, in which he envisioned a powerful submarine that can travel for many hours beneath the oceans—decades before the first deepwater submarines were deployed by the world's navies. And three years before Wells authored *The War of the Worlds*, he wrote another best seller, *The Time Machine*, which tells the story of a device that can carry a passenger into the past or future.

Still, by the end of the nineteenth century, few stories about alien visitors had found their way into popular culture. Although some authors had written stories about extraterrestrials and their civilizations before the publication of *The War of the Worlds*, most failed to gain widespread popularity among readers.

Social Commentaries

The earliest story about an extraterrestrial visitor, written around the ninth or tenth century, was a Japanese fairy tale known as *The Tale of the Bamboo Cutter*. The story tells the saga of a young child found by a lowly bamboo cutter who raises her as though she is his daughter. After the girl grows into a beautiful woman named Kaguya-hime (Japanese for "radiant night princess"), it is revealed that she is a princess from the moon and must return to her homeland.

In Europe a few writers speculated about alien civilizations, but their intent was mainly to provide political and social commentary about life on Earth. In 1656 Cyrano de Bergerac published the fantasy *Comical History of the States and Empires of the Moon*, in which a narrator travels to the moon in a ship propelled by firecrackers. The author intended the book to be pure satire. For example, the narrator finds that on the moon, money is not exchanged in the form of coins and paper currency, but in spoken words. Observes the narrator, "Thus when someone starves to death it is never but a blockhead and witty people always live off the fat of the land."[9]

> **DID YOU KNOW?**
>
> In the 1945 movie serial *The Purple Monster Strikes*, the Martian invader is a chameleonlike being, able to assume the physical identity of any creature on Earth.

The novella *Micromégas*, published by the French philosopher Voltaire in 1752, tells the story of two aliens, one 12,000 feet (3,658m) tall, the other 6,000 feet (1,829m) tall, who visit Earth, where they make some cogent observations about what they find. In one episode the two space travelers encounter a theologian who suggests that all creatures, planets, and stars are made for the pleasure of humans. The aliens find this notion laughable and reply that before they leave Earth they will author a book about philosophy that even tiny human minds can understand. After the extraterrestrials depart, the theologian opens the book and finds all the pages blank. Similar to the story concocted by Cyrano de Bergerac, Voltaire used extraterrestrials

Hugo Gernsback's *Amazing Stories*

Each year, the World Science Fiction Society presents the Hugo Awards to the writers of the year's best science fiction. The awards are named in honor of Hugo Gernsback, the first publisher of *Amazing Stories*.

Born in 1884 in Luxembourg, Gernsback immigrated to the United States in 1904. Gernsback invented components for 2-way radios and hoped to market them in America. To help sell radios, Gernsback established a magazine, *Modern Electronics*, giving tips to hobbyists on building and using the devices. In 1911, as Gernsback prepared an edition of the magazine for publication, he discovered several empty pages. To fill the pages, he sat down at a typewriter and cranked out a short science-fiction story, a tale about a future society titled "Ralph 124c 41+."

Readers responded enthusiastically, which prompted Gernsback to publish more fictional stories in his radio hobbyist's magazine. Finally, in 1926, Gernsback founded *Amazing Stories*, devoting the pulp magazine entirely to science fiction.

Gernsback was an ardent believer in life on other planets. "Chances overwhelmingly favor existence of life on Mars either past or present," Gernsback told his readers. To communicate with Martians, Gernsback proposed erection of a huge searchlight atop the world's tallest mountain, which he suggested the Martians could see from their home planet. He also believed beams of light could be used to transmit messages to Mars. "It is possible," he said, "that even today the Martians are using such a system to signal us." Gernsback died in 1967.

Quoted in Daniel Stashower, "A Dreamer Who Made Us Fall in Love with the Future," *Smithsonian,* August 1990, p. 44.

to make a social commentary about life on Earth—in this case, that tiny human brains are not capable of comprehending the vast complexities of the universe.

In 1854 French writer Charlemagne-Ischir Defontenay published one of the first novels about space travel that was not written in a satirical tone. In the book titled *Star*, Defontenay described an alien civilization on a planet he named Psi Cassiopeia. Among the inhabitants of the planet are humans as well as subhuman apelike creatures who toil as servants. Defontenay also described a species of 9-foot-tall (2.7m), blue-haired beings who are intellectually superior to humans and also immortal. During this era another French writer, Camille Flammarion, published two books, both speculating on life on other planets. One is a scientific tome, *The Plurality of Inhabited Worlds*, while the other is a work of fantasy, *The Inhabitants of the Other World*. "Beings may live and think organized altogether differently from those of your planet," Flammarion warns his readers. "The inhabitants of the other worlds have neither your form nor your senses. They are altogether different."[10]

Laying the Groundwork

There is a good reason these earliest books about extraterrestrials were written by authors like Defontenay and Flammarion. Both were men of science—Defontenay was a physician, and Flammarion studied astronomy. At the time, a wide knowledge of science was a necessary prerequisite for an author who wished to speculate on the possibility of life on other planets.

Before science-fiction writers could concoct stories about aliens and their civilizations, scientists had to lay the groundwork for the stories. For many centuries people believed in the biblical explanation for the birth of the universe. It took the work of astronomers such as Galileo, Johannes Kepler, and Nicolaus Copernicus to establish the existence of planets, thereby providing fiction writers places to base their alien civilizations.

Meanwhile, stories about alien races were largely made possible by the work of nineteenth-century British naturalist Charles Darwin, who conceived the theory of evolution. Before Darwin it was widely believed that humans, and all other living things, were made by God, and that humans were made in the image of God. Darwin wrote that humans and other living things evolved from lower forms of life through a natural process. With Darwin's viewpoint gaining traction in the public's mind, science-fiction writers began to speculate that other species could evolve elsewhere in the universe, on planets far away from Earth and under conditions that were not at all similar to those found on Earth.

Perhaps with more intense gravity than that found on Earth, the aliens would have evolved into beings the size of giants. Or with the surfaces of their planets completely submerged in water, the aliens would have evolved into a fishlike species. Says John Clute, "Evolution was necessary so that writers could begin to grasp the fact that different environments required different kinds of beings."[11]

Seeing Canals on Mars

Darwin's book, *On the Origin of Species*, was published in 1859. Meanwhile, astronomers were still making important discoveries about the environments and motions of the planets throughout the nineteenth century and into the early years of the twentieth century. As these discoveries were made and published, science-fiction writers took the facts available to them at the time, embellished them with their own ideas, and produced stories about alien civilizations.

Sometimes, it was the scientists—and not the science-fiction writers—whose beliefs about extraterrestrial life seemed as though they belonged more on the pages of novels than in textbooks. In the 1890s astronomer Percival Lowell peered at Mars through the eyepiece of his telescope and believed he saw canals—artificial waterways. Lowell insisted the canals had to have been built by an intelligent race of beings. Said Lowell, "To find, therefore, upon Mars highly intelligent life is what the planet's state would lead one to expect."[12] (In reality there are no canals on Mars. In later years astronomers speculated that Lowell was, well, seeing things.)

DID YOU KNOW?

A major Hollywood production of the John Carter stories is planned for 2012. *John Carter of Mars* will feature Canadian actor Taylor Kitsch, best known for his role in the TV drama *Friday Night Lights*.

Wells read Lowell's books and was inspired by the astronomer, but Wells's Martians were nothing like the beings envisioned by Lowell. Said the late Cornell University astronomer Carl Sagan, "Lowell's Martians were benign and hopeful, even a little god-like, very different from the malevolent menace posed by Wells."[13] Indeed, Wells's creatures were ugly, malicious, and relentless, written to shock the senses of his Victorian-era readers. In one scene Wells's narrator tells of watching a Martian devour a human.

Travels to Barsoom

The War of the Worlds proved to be enormously popular, receiving widespread praise from critics. Writing in the *Baltimore Sun*, one critic said, "There is nothing human about [Wells's] Martians; they are real, yet totally abnormal—abhorrent to us—while we crouch under their diabolic power."[14] Before its publication as a hardback book in America, many newspapers published the story in serial form. Each week, readers waited anxiously for the latest installment. The story was so popular that another author was commissioned to write a sequel even before the book was available in America.

Following publication of *The War of the Worlds*, many stories about alien invasions flooded the market, thanks in large part to the growth of the pulp magazine industry. (The genre was so named because of the cheap, pulp-like quality of the paper used in the publications.) The pulps included such periodicals as *Amazing Stories*, *Weird Tales*, and *Astounding Stories*.

One of the first pulps, *All-Story* magazine, made its debut in 1905. In 1912 the magazine featured the first of the John Carter stories written by Edgar Rice Burroughs, the author known mainly for his book *Tarzan of the Apes*. John Carter is an American adventurer who travels to Mars, finding a civilization of sword-fighting warriors. The stories were aimed

The Martian menace—ugly, malicious, and relentless—devours humans in its path in the 1898 novel War of the Worlds *by H.G. Wells. Wells's story was intended to shock the senses of his Victorian-era readers.*

at young readers enthralled with Carter's encounters with the kangaroo men of Gooli, the headless race of Martians known as the Rykors, the cave-dwelling Therns, the telepathic Lotharians, and other denizens of the planet, which Burroughs renamed Barsoom. Other characters include Carter's ally, the 13-foot-tall (4m) green-skinned Tars Tarkas, as well as the beautiful Dejah Thoris, princess of the Martian city Helium.

Publishers of other pulps saw the success of the John Carter stories and scrambled to find stories of alien civilizations for their own magazines. For the inaugural issue of *Amazing Stories* in 1926, publisher Hugo Gernsback included a story of alien invasion, "The Man Who Saved Earth," in which a scientist discovers a Martian plan to drain Earth's oceans. To further entice adolescent readers, *Amazing Stories* as well as the other pulps usually featured colorfully drawn covers illustrating the stories inside; many of the covers routinely depicted bug-eyed, snarling aliens carrying off helpless and frightened damsels.

A Hero Arrives

How long were Earthlings going to put up with hostile aliens invading their planet, bent on draining their oceans, kidnapping their women, and destroying their cities? On January 7, 1934, newspaper readers got their answer. That was the day artist Alex Raymond's comic strip, *Flash Gordon*, debuted in American newspapers. As the story unfolds, readers learn that a rogue planet, Mongo, is approaching Earth. Mongo's ruler, Ming the Merciless, intends to destroy humankind. The dashing and heroic Flash Gordon answers the call to duty. Accompanied by the beautiful Dale Arden and eccentric Dr. Hans Zarkov, Flash flies a spaceship to Mongo, where he matches wits with Ming while befriending or doing battle with all manner of extraterrestrial creatures he finds on the strange world: Lion Men, Shark Men, and Hawk Men, among others.

The Flash Gordon *comic strip, which debuted in US newspapers in 1934, saw its hero battling aliens bent on conquest and destruction. A 1938 movie serial chronicled the hero's exploits on Mars.*

YOUR FAVORITE NEWSPAPER ADVENTURE HERO ON THE SCREEN AGAIN!
UNIVERSAL INTERNATIONAL presents
FLASH GORDON'S TRIP TO MARS
with
LARRY "Buster" CRABBE
as FLASH GORDON
JEAN ROGERS
CHARLES MIDDLETON
FRANK SHANNON
BEATRICE ROBERTS
RICHARD ALEXANDER
MONTAGUE SHAW
15 THRILLING CHAPTERS
From the ALEX RAYMOND Newspaper Feature, owned and Copyrighted by KING FEATURES SYNDICATE INC

Raymond drew the strip for more than a decade. Other artists took over, drawing *Flash Gordon* until 2003, when the strip finally disappeared from newspaper comic pages. In the meantime, *Flash Gordon* was adapted into many other forms of entertainment. A radio serial was produced in 1935, followed a year later by a movie serial starring Buster Crabbe, a former Olympic swimmer, in the title role. The serial proved to be so popular that the studio produced a second *Flash Gordon* serial in 1938, chronicling Flash's adventures on Mars, and then a third serial in 1940, featuring a return trip to Mongo.

Fighting the Selenites

Movie serials like *Flash Gordon* were typically shown before the main features. Each week's episode spanned about 10 minutes, with each chapter ending in a cliffhanger, meaning that as the episode concluded, the heroes or heroines always found themselves in peril. To find out how Flash and his friends got themselves out of each week's jam, audience members would have to return for the next week's installment.

Adventure series featuring extraterrestrials proved to be popular among movie fans. In addition to the three *Flash Gordon* serials, during this era the studios also produced such serials as *Radar Men from the Moon*, *The Purple Monster Strikes*, and *Bruce Gentry—Daredevil of the Skies*. In all those serials, heroic protagonists battle evil alien invaders.

Plots centering on extraterrestrial encounters may have provided plenty of fodder for serials, but cinema audiences rarely saw stories about alien encounters as the main features. Indeed, as the pulp magazines churned out story after story, and as books about extrater-

> ### DID YOU KNOW?
>
> Flash Gordon was a hit among movie audiences and comic strip readers, but early efforts to adapt the character to pulp fiction failed. In 1936 *Flash Gordon Strange Adventure* magazine published just a single issue before folding.

The Predictions of George Tucker

An American politician, George Tucker, added to the list of satirical science fiction in 1827 when he published the novel *A Voyage to the Moon*. Tucker's novel about alien encounters on the moon is written with tongue planted firmly in cheek. However, writing more than 130 years before the era of spaceflight, Tucker made some predictions that ultimately proved to be quite accurate.

At the time, the concept of the airless vacuum of space was still quite foreign to many scientists, but Tucker suggested that his space travelers would have to be sealed in an airtight craft as they made their voyage. Moreover, Tucker's astronauts take along compressed air in tanks and also insulate their spacecraft against the cold temperatures of space—just as space travelers do today.

Tucker taught at the University of Virginia, where one of his students was Edgar Allan Poe, who would go on to become one of America's best-known writers of poetry, short fiction, and novels. Poe is known mostly for his suspense stories, but he did author one story about space travel, "The Unparalleled Adventures of One Hans Pfaal," which he published in 1835. Poe sends his astronaut to the moon in a balloon, theorizing that Earth's atmosphere extends all the way to its satellite.

restrial encounters flew off the shelves of bookstores, during the first half of the twentieth century, few feature-length movies about extraterrestrials were produced by the movie industry in Hollywood and elsewhere.

During this era, among the few feature-length films to focus on alien creatures was *Le Voyage dans la Lune* (in English, *A Trip to the Moon*) filmed by French cinema pioneer Georges Méliès in 1902. The story was cobbled together from two classic works of science fiction: the 1865 Jules Verne book *From the Earth to the Moon*, and a 1901 book by Wells, *First Men in the Moon*. In the story a group of five adventurers board a rocket that is shot to the moon by a huge cannon. After arriving on the moon, they exit the spacecraft—the Earth men find no need for spacesuits—and descend into a crater, where they discover a civilization of insect-like lunar inhabitants, the Selenites.

Down in the depths of the moon, a melee soon ensues as the explorers find themselves besieged by the Selenites. They discover their umbrellas make very good weapons—they learn that a poke with the pointy tip makes a Selenite explode into a cloud of dust. Still, it turns into a bit of a white-knuckle struggle, with the five travelers forced to scurry back to their spaceship just ahead of a mob of angry moon creatures. Unfortunately, one of the Earth men must stay behind to launch the ship back to the home planet. (Méliès does not let the audience in on his fate at the hands of the Selenites, but one can imagine the terrible doom he must have faced.) As for the others, they make it home safely and are welcomed as heroes.

Political Overtones

Over the next four decades, there would be few other attempts by filmmakers to produce mainstream feature films about extraterrestrial encounters—and those that were made often carried political or social overtones, much the same as the early extraterrestrial literature published years before. For example, the 1917 Danish movie *Himmelskibet* (in English, *The Airship*) features a voyage to Mars by the protagonist, Professor Planetarios, where he finds a race of white-robed, peace-loving

Human adventurers who reach the moon encounter hostile aliens with spiked heads and webbed feet with claws in Le Voyage dans la Lune (A Trip to the Moon), *a 1902 French film. The story combined elements of stories by Jules Verne and H.G. Wells.*

vegetarian mystics. Planetarios embraces their pacifism and returns to Earth to spread their message. After arriving home, Planetarios finds his campaign for peace resonating with the people of Earth, who drop their weapons and become friends. The film was produced as World War I raged in Europe, and so there is not much doubt about the message the filmmakers intended to send to audiences.

Another politically motivated science-fiction story can be found in *Aelita: Queen of Mars*, a Russian film produced with the blessing of the country's new Communist government. Released in 1924, the film tells the story of a scientist named Los who, frustrated with the political squabbling he finds on Earth, builds a spaceship and flies to Mars. After arriving on Mars, he meets the beautiful Martian queen, Aelita, whom he learns has been watching him through her telescope. As he falls in love with the queen of Mars, Los learns that her planet is no different than his: The workers are oppressed and talking revolution. The story ends as Los commits himself to the revolution—just as the Russians back home were expected to commit themselves to communism and the overthrow of the European monarchies.

For true science fiction, fans could always tune in their radios, which in 1938 featured the adaptation of *The War of the Worlds* that caused so much panic. Otherwise, by then Americans and other residents of the Western democracies had much more on their minds than Martians. Indeed, they were watching the skies, but not for alien spacecraft. World War II soon erupted. Filmmakers concentrated on the war effort, while pulp magazine publishers were forced to scale back (paper was in short supply due to wartime rationing). The aliens eventually returned to Earth, but not until the Germans and Japanese were vanquished.

CHAPTER TWO

They Come to Conquer

For the millions of teenagers who sit in class every day, wondering to themselves whether their teachers are truly from another planet, the producers of the 1998 film *The Faculty* attempted to provide the answer. And that answer is a definitive "Yes!"

The Faculty tells the story of six students who slowly realize their teachers are not who they purport to be; they are actually aliens who have arrived on Earth with the intention of conquering the human race. Their plan is simple: They are able to infect humans by inserting a parasitic organism into their ears, taking over the bodies of the hosts, who then spread the parasites to others. In the film the six students of Herrington High School in Ohio believe they have sniffed out the plan and concoct an inhaled drug that kills the parasites.

Film critics found much to enjoy about the film—mostly that it offers a clever twist on the old theme of teenage angst. Most movies and books about life in high school usually focus on the outsiders—the teenagers who do not fit in. In this story the outsiders are the teachers, and it is the popular kids, the cheerleaders and football stars, who expose their evil intentions. "It's an awfully enjoyable, hip little B-movie," wrote Salon.com film critic Charles Taylor. "It's almost subversive. That's school spirit I can get behind."[15]

Otherwise, there was not much else that was very original about *The Faculty*. Critics found it similar to the 1956 and 1978 productions of *Invasion of the Body Snatchers*, which tell the story of alien invaders who take over the bodies of humans as part of a diabolical plot to conquer the world. And well before those films were made, writers, filmmakers, and other creative people had conjured up many stories about visits by aliens that all share a common theme: When the extraterrestrials arrive, their intentions are always evil.

Flying Saucer Movies

Although there was certainly nothing very friendly about the aliens in *The War of the Worlds* or the *Flash Gordon* movie serials, the evilness of extraterrestrial visitors was ratcheted up a notch in the years following World War II. Starting in the early 1950s, movie studios churned out a long list of the so-called flying saucer movies, most of which featured alien invaders with ill intentions. Among these films were *Earth vs. the Flying Saucers*, *This Island Earth*, *Invasion of the Saucer-Men*, *Target Earth*, and the 1953 adaptation of *The War of the Worlds*. One of the most popular films from this era was the 1951 movie *The Thing from Another World*, based on the short story "Who Goes There?" by science-fiction writer Don A. Stuart.

The movie opens as an expedition of scientists and military members stationed at a remote Arctic outpost are dispatched to investigate what they believe is an airplane crash. Arriving at the scene by dogsled, the search party finds an object buried beneath the ice. Standing on the ice, the search party members can see a blurred image of the wreckage below their feet. Soon it becomes clear that they are not looking at an airplane,

> ### DID YOU KNOW?
>
> On the *X-Files*, the character Dana Scully was named in honor of author Frank Scully, who wrote the 1950 book *Behind the Flying Saucers*. The book attempted to prove the existence of extraterrestrial visitors.

INVASION OF THE SAUCER-MEN
starring
STEVE TERRELL · GLORIA CASTILLO · FRANK GORSHIN · Executive Producer SAMUEL Z. ARKOFF
Produced by JAMES H. NICHOLSON and ROBERT GURNEY Jr. · Directed by EDWARD L. CAHN · Screenplay by AL MARTIN
Additional Dialogue by ROBERT GURNEY Jr. · A MALIBU PRODUCTION · AN AMERICAN INTERNATIONAL PICTURE

Invasion of the Saucer-Men *was one of a string of flying saucer movies produced in the 1950s. Some of these movies, made around the time of the Korean War, reflected concerns about the spread of communism.*

but something they had not expected. "We finally got one," shouts one of the search party members, "We found a flying saucer!"[16]

After chopping through the ice to rescue the inhabitant of the crashed saucer, the rescuers find the alien to be not terribly appreciative of their efforts. After they take the disabled visitor back to their compound, the extraterrestrial—a combination vegetable and vampire dubbed "the Thing"—wakes up and goes into a murderous frenzy. He is finally subdued by the military members of the team, who rig a device that electrocutes the alien—despite the protests of a scientist who wants to communicate with the visitor. By the end of the film, audience members who sat through two terrifying hours of the Thing's rampage were probably in agreement with the military's solution. Says film historian Bruce Rux, "The Thing turns out to be a completely hostile entity, against which the military is shown to be wise in taking a hard and violent stance. The scientist in the movie is portrayed as foolish in his desire to learn more about the visitor, even if it should cost the lives of the entire Arctic party."[17]

More than a Story About Aliens

The movie was released just as American-led U.N. troops repelled the Communist Chinese and North Koreans who invaded South Korea. The Korean War had started the year before and initially had not gone well for the US-backed South Koreans, but when the American military regrouped and changed tactics, the Communists were made to retreat. Against this backdrop of world events, *The Thing from Another World* opened in American theaters. Clearly, the movie is intended as more than just a story about a hostile alien visitor. At the conclusion of the film, after the alien has been vanquished, newspaper reporter Ned Scott transmits the story to the world. Speaking into the radio transmitter from the remote Arctic outpost, Scott issues this warning: "Watch the skies . . . keep watching!"[18]

For what? Flying saucers? No, Scott's admonishment to Americans was meant to warn them against the likelihood of Communists invading California or Oregon, just as they had invaded South Korea. And if the Communists did invade, there would be no room for peaceful talk here—as that foolish scientist in the movie proposed. Instead, the wise course for Americans would be to repel them, just as US troops had repelled the Communists in South Korea, and just as the stalwart heroes in the Arctic repelled the vampire vegetable from outer space. Says Stephen King, "What do you do with a blood-drinking carrot from outer space? Simple. Cut him if he stands and shoot him if he runs."[19]

Small Screen Invaders

By the 1960s international communism still represented a threat to democracy, but science-fiction writers and filmmakers seemed content to

Can a Flying Saucer Really Fly?

Before World War II extraterrestrials in books and films traveled in ships propelled by rockets. This made sense at the time because that is how scientific visionaries such as Konstantin Tsiolkovsky in Russia, Robert Goddard in America, and Wernher von Braun in Germany predicted space travel would be accomplished. After World War II extraterrestrials on film and on TV started arriving in flying saucers, crafts that travel through space in clear defiance of the laws of physics.

The term "flying saucer" was concocted by newspapers, which reported the story told by pilot Kenneth Arnold, who claimed to have seen several airborne objects as he flew a small plane near Yakima, Washington, in June 1947. Arnold said the objects he saw "flew like a saucer would if you skipped it across water." Newspapers shortened that description to "flying saucer." Authors and filmmakers picked up the term and used it to envision vehicles capable of interplanetary travel.

As flights of NASA's Space Shuttle illustrate, it takes an enormous amount of fuel and thrust to break through Earth's gravity for a trip into space. A flying saucer would have no place to store all that fuel. Moreover, the pilot of a saucer would have little control over the craft once it entered Earth's atmosphere. A vehicle traveling through the air requires wings for lift and a tail to stabilize and steer the craft. Most flying saucers depicted on film and in literature have neither.

Quoted in Abe Dane, "Flying Saucers: The Real Story," *Popular Mechanics,* June 1995, p. 52.

let others explore political issues. Instead, they concentrated on weaving new stories about alien civilizations, concentrating on the fundamental premise that extraterrestrials are up to no good. The 1960s saw the premiere of the TV series *Lost in Space*, which told of the Robinsons, a space-faring family who encountered a different alien life-form each week. Some of the aliens were friendly, but most were not, and the story usually hinged on the abilities of 9-year-old Will Robinson and his robot sidekick to defeat the hostile creatures. Also during the 1960s, the series

The Invaders premiered, featuring a particularly sneaky race of extraterrestrials able to disguise themselves as humans.

Two other TV series that debuted in the 1960s include *Doctor Who* and *The Outer Limits*. A British import, *Doctor Who*—which continues to air today—frequently found the intrepid title character (who hails from a world far beyond Earth's solar system) matching wits with malevolent aliens both on Earth and on other worlds. Meanwhile, *The Outer Limits* was an anthology series, featuring a different set of characters and a different story each week. Many of the dramas featured humans responding to extraterrestrial threats. In fact, the opening narration of each show included a disembodied voice declaring that the aliens had already arrived and had taken over: "There is nothing wrong with your television. Do not attempt to adjust the picture. We are controlling transmission."[20]

> **DID YOU KNOW?**
>
> *Doctor Who* premiered on British TV in 1963; since then 11 actors have portrayed the doctor who can travel through space and time.

By the 1970s a new form of entertainment had been introduced to the American public: the video game. Game producers quickly adapted the alien invasion theme—one of the first and most successful games of the era was *Space Invaders*. By today's standards, the game's graphics were rudimentary: Essentially, the game consisted of rows of aliens slowly descending on a city while the player picked them off with an electronic cannon. At first, arcade versions of *Space Invaders* could be found in bars and bowling alleys, where millions of dedicated players poured their quarters into the machines. Eventually, the American game company Atari produced a home version of the game.

As the graphics and computer power behind the games improved, game developers returned often to the theme of alien invasion. Among the most popular games to have been released in recent years are *Destroy All Humans!*, *Corridor 7: Alien Invasion*, and *Half-Life 2*. These games are highly addictive. The series of *Halo* games introduced in 2001 has earned its producers profits of nearly $2 billion. The *Halo* game scenarios follow the adventures of an alien hunter, the Master Chief, as he obliterates malicious extraterrestrials who belong to a dark alliance known as the Covenant. The latest game in the series, *Halo: Reach*, was made available in 2010—earning more than $200 million in sales on the first day of its release.

The *Halo* games as well as the others are among the class of video games known as first-person shooter games, meaning they require the player to blast away at the invading extraterrestrials. Even with improved graphics and vastly more powerful computer chips controlling the action, the basic scenario of the alien invasion video game does not appear to have changed since the *Space Invaders* era.

Video games such as Halo: Reach, *released in 2010, are among the more recent examples of how space aliens have invaded pop culture. The popular* Halo *series revolves around the adventures of an alien hunter who obliterates malicious extraterrestrials at every opportunity.*

Big Budgets and Big Stars

By the 1980s many filmmakers had concluded that TV and movie fans were similar to video game players—they wanted to see lots of action. Producers delivered action-packed titles such as *Species, Mars Attacks, Independence Day, Alien* and its sequels, *Predator* and its sequels, and remakes of *The Thing from Another World* and *The War of the Worlds*. All these films featured plots centering on invasions by evil extraterrestrials, and they all came with big budgets, state-of-the-art special effects, and major stars. It might be hard to imagine stars of the caliber of Sigourney Weaver, Will Smith, Jeff Goldblum, and Tom Cruise appearing in the flying saucer movies of the 1950s. But given the enormous box-office appeal of alien invasion films by the late twentieth century, producers seemed to have little trouble convincing Hollywood's biggest names to lend their talents to alien invasion films.

> ### DID YOU KNOW?
>
> Since the first *Halo* title was released in 2001, more than 34 million units of the game and its sequels have been sold worldwide.

Independence Day, which was released in 1996, was among the most successful films of this era, chalking up international box-office receipts of more than $800 million. Within the first few minutes of the film, the aliens make their presence known on Earth, and they also make their intentions known. The malevolent alien warmongers position their huge spacecraft above the White House, then blast the executive mansion to pieces. The visitors follow up that horrific act with a relentless campaign to kill, destroy, and conquer. The only mystery remaining is how the people of Earth will eventually outsmart the aliens (which they do).

"The Truth Is Out There"

Not all alien threats hover overhead in gravity-defying warships. As FBI agents Fox Mulder and Dana Scully discover in the long-running TV series *The X-Files*, the aliens often walk among us and, furthermore, the

US government knows about them and carefully guards the secret of their presence.

The series, which debuted on American TV in 1992, described the adventures of the two FBI agents assigned to a category of cases known as the X-Files—unsolved mysteries involving paranormal activity. Scully, trained as a physician, is the skeptic of the team, but Mulder is convinced that alien invaders are behind the mysteries and, in fact, believes his sister was abducted by extraterrestrials. Each week Mulder and Scully attempted to unravel the creepy mysteries, often finding themselves thwarted by a shadowy government entity known as the Syndicate that is protecting the aliens and their ultimate goal of taking over the world. As the *X-Files* repeatedly warned audience members, "The truth is out there."

Mulder and Scully pursued their alien antagonists across the country. In Iowa they found them at a zoo, herding animals onto an intergalactic Noah's Ark. In Pennsylvania they found them impersonating Amish farmers. In Florida they found extraterrestrials posing as circus performers. One episode found audience members squirming as robot cockroaches are dispatched by the invaders to kill the people of Earth. "Anyone who thinks alien visitation will come not in the form of robots, but in living beings with big eyes and gray skin, has been brainwashed by too much science fiction,"[21] a robotics expert warns Mulder.

The series turned out to be enormously popular, remaining on the air for 12 seasons while spawning a 1998 theatrical film version, *The X-Files: Fight the Future*. Millions of people, known among themselves as "X-Philes," became devoted fans. Fans in most American cities formed clubs and met regularly to watch videotapes of favorite episodes and to trade *X-Files* show gossip and theories about plots and characters. "Some

Big-budget, big-action alien invasion films caught on in the 1980s. The 1987 film Predator (a scene from the movie is pictured) was one of these. Plots centered on evil extraterrestrials wreaking havoc on Earth.

people can get kind of weird and obsessed, but we aren't freaks,"[22] insisted Kristin Vogel, a St. Louis, Missouri, X-Phile. Some clubs staged annual X-Phile conventions, drawing fans from across the country. At many conventions, a popular exhibit featured a mockup of Mulder's office in the basement of FBI headquarters. Fans could get their pictures taken behind Mulder's desk, tossing pencils at the ceiling (as Mulder often did when he was bored and frustrated).

The Internet became a major factor in promoting interest in the show. X-Philes developed their own fan pages, promoting ideas about the characters and plots. They puzzled over burning questions such as who were the computer experts that helped Mulder break into computer files, who was the creepy character that crawled through drainpipes, who was the Cigarette Smoking Man, and what was the black ooze? Fans provided their own opinions on their pages, started blogs, and published their own online fan fiction using the characters from the show to concoct their stories. Within five years of the show's debut, the *Wall Street Journal* estimated that nearly 1,000 fan sites had been dedicated to the *X-Files*.

Although the show featured likeable and attractive stars in David Duchovny and Gillian Anderson, as well as strong writing and weird plots, the real appeal was its creepiness and how it left viewers anxious and uneasy. Says author and University of Wisconsin philosophy professor Mark C.E. Peterson:

> It is chock-a-block with gloom, desperation, surreal characters, and the anxiety of being on the threshold of the terrible secret. The anxiety in this case is not merely that there are aliens, scary enough on its own, but that this urgent "truth" has been intentionally withheld by a conspiracy of dangerous people. So long as the truth is kept from us, so long as we do not have it, we must live in service to a truth provided *by someone else*, and thus our lives will be lived, not on our terms, but on the terms of whoever provides that truth.[23]

The Worst Movie . . . Ever

When film historians compile lists of the worst movies ever made, one movie frequently earns the top spot on those lists: *Plan 9 from Outer Space*. Released in 1959 by director Edward D. Wood Jr., the story centers on an alien plot to resurrect the dead, turning them into zombies. The movie was made on a shoestring budget with the most rudimentary of special effects: The strings holding the miniature flying saucers are clearly visible on camera. To star in the film, Wood drafted such acting-challenged celebrities as Tor Johnson, a 400-pound (181kg) professional wrestler from Sweden; and Maili Nurmi, better known as Vampira, the sultry host of a weekly fright flick program on Los Angeles TV. Another featured player was the veteran actor Bela Lugosi, who died 3 years before filming began. Wood had shot footage of the aging horror film star and spliced it into *Plan 9*.

Says film critic David Denby, "In the ironic pantheon of film trivia–schlock, the films of Edward D. Wood Jr. inhabit a special place. Such Wood movies as . . . *Plan 9 From Outer Space* are so bad that they seem to undermine the film medium altogether. For people who attend festivals of 'worst films,' Wood may be no more than a proud hero of terribleness."

David Denby, "Distressed Woody," *New York*, October 17, 1994, p. 71.

More Alien Battles to Come

In the twenty-first century, authors and filmmakers continue to return again and again to the concept that aliens have come to Earth to conquer. Among the recent novels to explore this concept have been Adam Roberts's *Yellow Blue Tibia*, which suggests that an alien attack may have been at the root of the 1986 Chernobyl nuclear plant disaster in Ukraine, and Carol Emshwiller's *The Mount*, which tells the story of an Earth under the conquest of aliens who keep people as pets.

On TV, *Doctor Who* is expected to be around for many more seasons, while video game executives are planning new incarnations of the *Halo* series. What is more, a film version of *Halo* is in development with a possible release in 2012.

Other new films exploring Earth's testy relations with extraterrestrial visitors include *The Darkest Hour* and *Battle: Los Angeles*, both of which are scheduled for release in 2011. *The Darkest Hour* tells the story of a group of Americans trapped in Russia during an alien invasion. In *Battle: Los Angeles*, the action occurs closer to home. According to the plot, US marines are called in to fight an alien invasion on the streets of Los Angeles.

Director Jonathan Liebesman says his inspiration for *Battle: Los Angeles* came largely from the news footage of American troops fighting insurgents on city streets in Iraq and Afghanistan. "I found a lot of the embedded footage of the marines in Iraq and Afghanistan incredibly powerful," says Liebesman, "and I thought that would just be a great way to tell an alien invasion story."[24]

> ## DID YOU KNOW?
>
> In the 2011 film *Battle: Los Angeles*, a false sighting of Japanese invaders that prompted antiaircraft fire over the city during World War II is portrayed as a scouting mission by aliens planning their modern-day invasion.

Movies like *Battle: Los Angeles* and *The Darkest Hour* are bound to appeal to the popular imagination. As many filmmakers, authors, game designers, and other creative people have learned, Americans love extraterrestrials, especially those who want to conquer and enslave them.

CHAPTER THREE

They Come in Peace

Paul is no ordinary extraterrestrial. For starters, he did not come to Earth to conquer but, rather, in search of a good time. Things did not exactly work out for Paul, though, and soon after arriving he found himself a prisoner of the US government, which hid him away in a secret laboratory in the notorious Area 51.

Area 51 is part of a US military base located deep in the Nevada desert. For decades UFO believers have suspected that the government has hidden evidence of alien visitors in Area 51. In the film *Paul*, slated for release in 2011, two goofy comic book fans, Graeme and Clive, decide to explore Area 51 for themselves. Just as they arrive, Paul the extraterrestrial manages to make his escape from Area 51. He appeals to Graeme and Clive for assistance, and the friends agree to help Paul make his way to a waiting mother ship so he may return to his home planet.

Paul may not be Ming the Merciless or even the Thing, but he is certainly not E.T., the lovable and lost alien visitor from the hit 1982 film *E.T.: The Extraterrestrial*. In the film, Paul is a wisecracking, fun-loving alien with an attitude. "[Paul] is the cool older friend," says the film's director, Greg Mottola, "but he's also kind of crass and childish. We're making an attempt to move him away from the . . . E.T. model."[25]

Religious Themes

Paul is among many films, books, and short stories that have portrayed aliens not as malevolent conquerors but, rather, as friendly visitors who come in peace (or, in Paul's case, in search of a good time). Dating back to the earliest days of science fiction, many writers have speculated that aliens may be friendly visitors who come to Earth with good intentions.

Even during the flying saucer era of the 1950s, some filmmakers resisted the temptation to portray all aliens as evil and bloodthirsty. In the 1951 film *The Day the Earth Stood Still*, the alien Klaatu arrives in a flying saucer in broad daylight, landing in a park in Washington, D.C., just a few blocks from the White House. His intention is to warn the people of Earth to cease their self-destructive tendencies. The issue that concerned Klaatu was the proliferation of nuclear weapons; the alien feared Earth would deploy the weapons in space and endanger other worlds.

Religious themes are woven throughout the story. Klaatu is portrayed by rail-thin British actor Michael Rennie. He soon emerges as a Christlike figure—escaping from army custody, Klaatu presents himself at a boarding house as a man named Carpenter. Moreover, near the end of the film, Klaatu is shot and killed by the military, but his robot companion manages to bring the alien back to life temporarily—resurrecting Klaatu—so that he may deliver his final words of warning to the people of Earth.

Having spoken his last words—threatening them with annihilation unless they cease development of nuclear weapons—Klaatu returns to his ship and rises to the heavens. Says John Clute:

> Nobody who saw it in 1951 ever forgot it, and it is still a film one returns to with nostalgia and fright. A flying saucer lands in Washington, D.C., and a great robot and a human emerge. The human tells Earth governments to behave, or they will be blown away. The human is duly murdered by us. The robot . . . gives him rebirth. His disappointment in humankind is infectious.[26]

Environmental Concerns Surface

The film was remade and released in 2008. This time Klaatu tells the people of Earth that he is concerned about the environmental destruction of the planet and warns world leaders that their abuses of the environment will not be tolerated. Klaatu, this time portrayed by Keanu Reeves, says he represents several alien civilizations who guard the well-being of planets capable of supporting life—of which Earth is one of only a few in the universe. "We can't let the Earth die," Klaatu tells a scientist. "It's one of the only planets that can support life."[27]

Religious themes again dominate the plot, but this time Klaatu is not Christ; he is Noah. As the story unfolds, world leaders learn that Klaatu is organizing a roundup of representatives of all plant and animal species on Earth, which he commences transporting into space. In the Old Testament story, God washed away the sins of civilization by commanding flood waters to rise. In the 2008 version of *The Day the Earth Stood Still*, Klaatu intends a similar obliteration of the human species on Earth. But as the alien mingles with the people of Earth, he discovers their moral spirit and love for one another and calls off the plan. "The intent of this was not to deliver a message. It was to deliver a picture of where we are," says the film's director, Scott Derrickson. "The issues that the movie is talking about, all the crises that we're in—the military crisis, the financial crisis, the environmental crisis—solving those problems will come at a price; they will demand sacrifice."[28]

Grave Misunderstandings

Antiwar themes as well as predictions of environmental catastrophe have found their way into other stories about alien visits. In the 1960s, as environmental preservation and antiwar sentiments emerged as important national issues, author Walter Tevis published *The Man Who Fell to*

The Fathers of Superman

According to the saga of Superman, the character's father is Jor-El, a citizen of the planet Krypton who saves his young son from the demise of the planet by sending him to Earth in a spaceship. In reality, Superman has two fathers—two young men from Cleveland, Ohio.

Jerry Siegel and Joe Shuster, both born in 1914, met at Glenville High School in Cleveland and became instant friends. Both were avid readers of *Amazing Stories* and other pulp magazines and shared an interest in science fiction. They were also fans of the newspaper comic strips featuring Tarzan, the African jungle king, and Buck Rogers, a twenty-fifth-century adventurer. The two friends worked closely together on the Glenville student newspaper, where Shuster drew cartoons and Siegel wrote humorous stories.

Away from school, they toyed with the idea of creating their own comic strip featuring a hero with super powers. Over time, the character of Superman evolved, but it took until 1938 for Siegel and Shuster to sell the idea to a publisher. The first Superman story was released in August 1938 under the title *Action Comics*. Siegel recalled that the comic book was an instant success. He said, "The publishers themselves didn't quite realize the power of Superman until they learned that at the newsstand people were asking not for *Action Comics,* but for the magazine with Superman in it." Siegel died in 1996; Shuster died in 1992.

Quoted in Les Daniels, *Superman: The Complete History—the Life and Times of the Man of Steel.* San Francisco: Chronicle, 2004, p. 35.

Earth. The novel, which was adapted into a 1976 theatrical movie and 1987 made-for-TV film, tells the story of an alien named Newton who leaves his home planet of Anthea in search of water. On Anthea nuclear war has obliterated the planet's population, leaving just a few dozen survivors, who are running out of water. After arriving on Earth, Newton plans to use his superior intellect to build a spaceship that can return to Anthea to save the remaining members of his race. As Newton carries out his plan, his true identity is discovered by sinister forces within the

US government who misinterpret his intentions, believing them to be hostile. His plans ruined, Newton is forced to remain on Earth while the population of Anthea dies off.

An even graver misunderstanding of alien intentions can be found in an episode of a 1990s revival of the *Outer Limits* TV show titled "Trial by Fire." The episode follows the story of a new president, who learns a fleet of alien spaceships is approaching Earth. The president is torn between his instincts, which suggest to him that the aliens are friendly, and military leaders, who warn him to prepare for attack. As the tension builds, a message from the alien fleet is received on Earth.

Cryptologists are put to work to decode the message. In the meantime, the fleet draws closer. Finally, the president caves in to the military and orders a nuclear missile fired toward the alien ships. The aliens intercept the missile, though, and blast it out of space. The alien visitors, fearing the intentions of the people of Earth, launch their own bombs, with one aimed directly at Washington, D.C. With seconds remaining before the bombs hit, the cryptologists deliver the decoded message. It says, "Let us be your friends."[29]

Connecting with Aliens

The military was also unduly suspicious of the aliens in two very popular films of the 1970s and 1980s: *Close Encounters of the Third Kind* (1977) and *E.T.: The Extraterrestrial* (1982). In both cases, though, the better angels of human nature prevailed, and the visitors in each story received warm welcomes and pleasant send-offs.

Close Encounters of the Third Kind was written and produced specifically to tap into the mysteries surrounding people who claim to have seen unidentified flying objects. According to criteria established by the late UFO investigator J. Allen Hynek, a close encounter of the first kind is an

The possibility of peaceful interaction with extraterrestrials is explored in the popular 1977 film Close Encounters of the Third Kind. *In this scene from the movie, an alien craft lands at Devils Tower National Monument in Wyoming as onlookers watch the historic event.*

DID YOU KNOW?

Before filming began, NASA asked *Close Encounters of the Third Kind* director Steven Spielberg to kill the movie. Spielberg says NASA's request indicates the agency knows something about extraterrestrials it does not want the public to learn.

encounter with a UFO in which the object is identified as an alien spacecraft by the witness. A close encounter of the second kind is an encounter with a UFO in which physical evidence is left behind—such as scorched grassland or crop fields where the UFO landed or power interruptions caused by the magnetic field created by the flight of the craft. A close encounter of the third kind occurs when the witness reports visual contact with the occupant of a UFO.

The story follows two people, power company worker Roy Neary and single mother Jillian Guiler, as they experience close encounters of the second kind with alien spaceships, then follow a mysterious attraction that leads them to Devils Tower, a 1,200-foot-tall (366m) column of rock in Wyoming. Neary walks out on his family and job in pursuit of the extraterrestrials, while Guiler follows the trail to retrieve her young son, who has been abducted by the aliens. As they dodge military patrols and make their way to the top of the column, Neary and Guiler discover that a landing zone has been set up to welcome the alien ship.

When the alien ship arrives, it frees Guiler's son and other abductees. Neary is welcomed aboard by the tiny and frail creatures, and he opts to leave his life on Earth to explore a new world. Says the film's director, Steven Spielberg, "He goes into the ship knowing what he's doing. He makes the most important decision in the history of the world."[30]

Psychic Bonds

Spielberg also directed *E.T.: The Extraterrestrial*, another film that revolves around a friendly alien visitor. As in *Close Encounters*, Spielberg again explored some of the mysteries surrounding the cult of UFO believers—specifically, the claim by many that they have formed bonds with aliens they encountered.

In *E.T.* the story opens as an alien spaceship lands in a California forest but is forced to make a quick getaway—some nosy government agents are on the trail—leaving behind a member of the crew. Stranded

A young boy befriends an alien who is accidentally stranded on Earth in the 1982 movie E.T.: The Extraterrestrial. *The movie suggests that bonds between earthly and extraterrestrial civilizations are possible.*

The Close Encounters of J. Allen Hynek

Director Steven Spielberg based his film *Close Encounters of the Third Kind* on the work of UFO investigator J. Allen Hynek, who coined the term that became the title for the film. The term is used to describe a human encounter with an extraterrestrial being.

The longtime chair of the Department of Astronomy at Northwestern University in Illinois, Hynek developed an interest in UFO studies after he was asked to investigate a series of sightings in Michigan. After interviewing several people, Hynek concluded that the witnesses had been mistaken and that the strange lights in the sky they saw were due to natural phenomena. Nevertheless, Hynek predicted that humans would one day encounter extraterrestrial visitors. "Scientists in the year 2066 may think us very naïve in our denials," he said.

Hynek went on to found the Center for UFO Studies, based in Chicago, Illinois, and served as a consultant to the US Air Force until the military gave up investigating UFO sightings in 1969. Still, Hynek pursued many UFO investigations on his own until his death in 1986. Said Hynek, "If I can succeed in making the study of UFOs scientifically respectable and do something constructive in it, then I think that would be a real contribution."

Quoted in Joan Cook, "J. Allen Hynek, Astronomer and UFO Consultant, Dies," *New York Times,* May 1, 1986, p. D-27.

on Earth, the extraterrestrial soon meets a young boy named Elliott, who takes the visitor home and hides him from authorities.

Elliott names the visitor E.T. and forms a bond with the alien—the two develop a psychic connection. Says Bruce Rux, "E.T. and his young personal friend, Elliott, are so psychically linked in the movie that each feels the other's emotions at all times, and Elliott can sense what the alien is thinking as well, serving as a personal translator when the government moves in on them."[31]

Eventually, Elliott helps E.T. make contact with his ship. A rendezvous is arranged, and E.T. manages to escape just one step ahead of the government agents. If films such as *Close Encounters of the Third Kind* and *E.T.: The Extraterrestrial* prove anything, it is that when ordinary people like Roy Neary and Elliott are able to make contact with the aliens, things go well and a bond is formed between civilizations. But when presidents and military leaders make first contact, the stories frequently end in bombs going off.

The Ultimate Alien Do-Gooder

E.T. and the aliens from *Close Encounters* were just visiting—not really here to do much more than just look around. Paul the alien arrived on Earth searching for a good time. Other aliens who have visited Earth have resolved to be of far more assistance to the human race.

On the planet Krypton, which was facing destruction, Jor-El placed his infant son Kal-El into a spaceship and sent him to Earth. Years later the tiny craft crashed into a farm field in Kansas. The surprised farmers, Ma and Pa Kent, find the child and raise the boy as their own. As he grows older, Clark Kent learns he possesses superhuman powers—super strength, X-ray vision, invulnerability, and the power to fly—and vows to use his gifts to fight crime and otherwise help humankind. He assumes the role of Superman.

Actually, Superman was not born on Krypton but in Cleveland, Ohio. That is where two friends, writer Jerry Siegel and artist Joe Shuster, conceived the character in 1933. It took five years for the two friends to sell their idea to a publisher, but finally, in 1938, Superman made his first appearance in a comic book titled *Action Comics*.

> **DID YOU KNOW?**
>
> A graphic novel series titled *Superman: The Dark Side* explores what would have occurred if Kal-El's ship had landed on the war-torn planet Apokolips. In the story Kal-El uses his super powers to obliterate his enemies.

Superman's story has never grown old. It has been adapted into a variety of media—books, TV shows, films, video games, and even a Broadway musical. Author and media historian Les Daniels says a character of Superman's moral resolve—always to do good—could not have been born on Earth. It is simply not normal for a human never to harbor dark thoughts or intentions—that is part of being human. Therefore, Superman had to come from someplace else, which means he had to come from a place where human frailties do not exist—a place like the planet Krypton.

Alien Savior

Superman arrived in an era of dangerous fascism—just three years after Superman's debut, the United States would find itself at war against Nazi Germany and Imperial Japan. Daniels says it took an outsider, an extraterrestrial, to rise above the moral failings of humans. And in the years since his debut, Superman has remained essentially the same character throughout all manner of national and international crises—through the Vietnam War, the Watergate scandal, the terrorist attacks of 2001, and the wars in Iraq and Afghanistan.

Humans may have made some terrible decisions during those crises, but Superman never lost his values, and he remained dedicated to the same cause that his creators envisioned nearly 80 years ago. Says Daniels:

Siegel had previously envisioned mighty men who were fools or fiends, but with the new Superman he had a hero who was not entirely human, and thus might logically be immune to human weaknesses. In presenting an otherworldly being, Siegel seems to have touched on a mythic theme of universal significance. Superman [was] Moses, set adrift to become his people's savior, and also Jesus, sent from above to redeem the world. There are parallel stories in many cultures, but what is significant is that Siegel, working in the . . . medium of comics, had created a secular American messiah.[32]

By the early twenty-first century, Superman's story continued to be told in many media—a new film version, *Superman Returns*, was released in 2006, while comic books, graphic novels, animated versions, TV series, and video games featuring the character are constantly in production. Through it all, Superman has stood steadfast, remaining a hero to all—proving that some aliens do come in peace.

CHAPTER FOUR

Off-World Encounters

The last time space travelers left Earth's orbit and headed to another body in space was in the late 1960s and early 1970s during the Apollo moon program. After launch, it took about 4 days for the Apollo missions to travel to the moon, which is roughly 250,000 miles (402,336km) from Earth. Therefore, an Apollo spacecraft could travel about 62,500 miles (100,584km) per day.

Physicists know that is not fast enough to achieve interstellar travel. Stars are separated by vast distances—tens of trillions of miles. To explore distant planets, spaceships need to travel faster than the speed of light. That type of travel would violate the laws of physics—unless, of course, the ship possesses a warp drive.

Warp Drive and First Contact

A warp drive would bend, or warp, space. The ship's engines then power through this bent chunk of space, enabling the craft to arrive at a destination trillions of miles away in a very short amount of time—often within a few moments.

At the present time, there are no warp drives. Fans of *Star Trek* know, however, that the warp drive will be invented in 2061 by eccentric scientist Zefram Cochrane, who will launch the first starship, the *Phoenix*, from an abandoned missile silo in Montana. During the test flight, Cochrane will make contact with a passing ship piloted by members of an alien race, the Vulcans.

By the twenty-third century, warp drives will be important components of the ships that travel under the authority of the United Federation of Planets. One of those vessels is the starship *Enterprise*. During the opening narration for *Star Trek*, the ship's commander, Captain James Tiberius Kirk, intones the mission of the *Enterprise*: "To explore strange new worlds. To seek out new life and new civilizations. To boldly go where no man has gone before."[33]

Saga of the *Enterprise*

Since its debut on American TV in 1966, *Star Trek* has set the standard for stories that focus on human exploration of space and encounters with alien civilizations. After the 3-year run of the initial series, the *Star Trek* story was adapted into 4 other TV series, as well as a series of books and films, the last of which was released in 2009. That film, titled *Star Trek*, traced the story from the characters' youthful days, when they were just starting their careers as young officers aboard the *Enterprise*. The success of the film illustrated that more than 4 decades after the original series premiered on TV, audiences are still drawn to the saga of the *Enterprise* and its crew. Worldwide, the film earned nearly $400 million in box-office sales. A sequel is planned for 2012.

Over the years, the various crews of the *Enterprise* have encountered all manner of alien civilizations—some primitive, some hostile, some friendly. Among them are the Mugatos, ill-tempered and resembling apes, who also sport poisonous fangs and horns extending from

> ### DID YOU KNOW?
>
> During the opening narration of the original *Star Trek* series, Captain Kirk explains the *Enterprise* is on a five-year mission to explore new worlds; in reality the NBC network canceled the series after three years.

The Star Trek *universe has populated television, movies, and books for several decades. The Klingons are one of many civilizations found in this universe. Pictured here is the Klingon ambassador from the 1986 film* Star Trek IV: The Voyage Home.

the tops of their heads; Tellarites, stubborn and argumentative, who truly are pigheaded (their heads resembled those of pigs); the Gorn, a race of warriors, who resemble lizards on two legs; and the Andorians, blue skinned and sporting antennae and white hair. The *Enterprise* crew mistakenly takes the Andorians for granted, underestimating their capacity for violence.

Aliens with Human Qualities

In all versions of *Star Trek*, the alien races given the most focus are the Vulcans and Klingons. Vulcans are a peaceful race known for their intelligence and skills in diplomacy. Vulcans resemble humans save for their green-tinted skin, pointy ears, and sloping eyebrows. The best-known Vulcan is Spock, a graduate of Starfleet Academy and first officer aboard the *Enterprise*.

The Klingons are a warrior people and maintain an icy relationship with the Federation. Physically, they are humanoid as well, resembling Mongols from the era of the conqueror Genghis Khan.

Many fans have been drawn into the *Star Trek* universe specifically because the creators have made the Vulcans and Klingons almost like real people. In 1991 the magazine *New Scientist* conducted a poll among scientists and found that many believed *Star Trek* demonstrates that science does have a human face (albeit one

DID YOU KNOW?

According to film historian Bruce Rux, there are more than 70 million copies of *Star Trek* books in print, with 13 copies sold every minute in America. The books have been translated into 15 languages, including Chinese and Hebrew.

that may have pointy ears) and that the TV shows, films, and books in the series have helped show that science is about more than just test tubes and microscope slides. Write authors and cultural studies professors Henry Jenkins and John Tulloch, "*Star Trek* is confirmation that what they are doing is worthwhile, that science is not an unnatural, sinister art that will lead to our destruction, but something that will allow us to become richer, fuller humans."[34]

Invasion of the Trekkers

Star Trek has evolved into something more than a TV show and series of movies. Just as the *X-Files* spawned a generation of X-Philes, in the years after production of the original *Star Trek* series, millions of fans have proudly declared themselves "Trekkers" (or, as others may call them, somewhat derisively, "Trekkies"). There are more than 500 local clubs of *Star Trek* fans in America and other countries. Many fans attend annual conventions in which they dress in the uniforms of the *Enterprise* crew or as aliens who have been featured over the years.

Time magazine said of these *Star Trek* fans:

> They're the ones who debate for hours the merits of the episode in which Mr. Spock mind-melded with a bloblike alien called the Horta. . . . They know the scientific properties of dilithium crystals, they have memorized the floorplan of the starship *Enterprise*, and they can say, "Surrender or die!" in the Klingon language. They have immersed themselves, with a fervor matched by few devotees of any religious sect, in a fully imagined future world.[35]

Jonathan Frakes, who portrayed Commander William Riker on the spinoff TV series *Star Trek: The Next Generation*, recalled his experience signing autographs at one Trekkers' convention: "I get very nervous when they ask me questions about the show, because they all know more information about it than I do."[36]

The influence of *Star Trek* on American pop culture extends beyond the annual Trekker conventions. In 1976 *Star Trek* fans organized a letter-writing campaign that convinced NASA to name the first space shuttle the *Enterprise*. Meanwhile, a 14-foot (4.3m) model of the starship *Enterprise* hangs in the Smithsonian Institution in Washington, D.C. At the Universal Studios tour in Hollywood, the most popular exhibit is a mockup of the *Enterprise* control room. The town of Riverside, Iowa, has issued a city proclamation declaring itself the birthplace of Captain Kirk. (Actually, the proclamation declares itself the *future* birthplace of the *Star Trek* hero, inasmuch as Kirk will not be born until the year 2233.) Even casual fans of the show know that Klingons enjoy Shakespeare (as long as they can read the works of the Bard in the Klingon language) and that Vulcans always part company with these warm words to one another: "Live long and prosper."

The *Star Wars* Saga

As *Star Trek* fans have remained devoted to the ongoing saga of Kirk and Spock, a sort of parallel universe has been created by fans of the *Star Wars* films. Since the release of the first film in 1977, millions of fans have followed the exploits of Luke Skywalker, Han Solo, Princess Leia, Obi-Wan Kenobi, and Padmé Amidala. As any *Star Trek* fan knows, the Klingons are not exactly at war with the Federation. In *Star Trek* the political situation that exists between the Federation planets and the Klingons is portrayed similar to the Cold War era on Earth, when the relationship between the United States and the former Soviet Union was often quite icy. In *Star Trek* each side tries to undermine the other, but battles between the Klingon vessels known as Birds of Prey and Federation starships are rare. In contrast, there is no doubt about the relations maintained between the forces of the Galactic Empire and the Rebel Alliance in the series of *Star Wars* films.

They are engaged in a long-running war that has spanned six films dating back to 1977. The latest film, *Revenge of the Sith*, was released in

The *Star Wars* Cantina Scene

Among all the aliens depicted in the seven *Star Wars* films, the extraterrestrials featured in the cantina scene in the original 1977 film stand out as some of the most unusual creatures to have appeared on film. In the scene young Luke Skywalker and Jedi master Obi-Wan Kenobi have entered a cantina on the planet Tatooine in search of a pilot who will fly them to the planet Alderaan, where they can join the Rebel Alliance. Inside, they find all manner of bug-eyed aliens and hammer-headed extraterrestrials, most with protruding fangs, horns, fins, tentacles, and other weird body parts.

Originally, the script called for seven aliens in the cantina, but director George Lucas permitted the film's monster makers to let their imaginations run wild, and by the time shooting started, there were 25 aliens created for the scene. Four of the aliens are members of a combo that provides music for the cantina patrons. Said Jon Berg, one of the designers who created the aliens for the film, "George showed us a cut of the cantina sequence . . . and it was just really exciting. This was the movie we'd all wanted to see, and here it was happening right in front of us."

Quoted in J.W. Rinzler, *The Making of Star Wars.* New York: Ballantine, 2007, p. 113.

2005. The six films as well as an animated feature, *The Clone Wars*, have earned total worldwide box-office receipts of more than $4 billion. In the meantime, the series has spawned dozens of books, TV series, radio dramas, and video games.

During the era of the *Star Wars* adventures, the human characters interact with alien life-forms. Unlike *Star Trek*, in which the mission of the *Enterprise* is to seek out new life and new civilizations, the alien life that populates the planets in the *Star Wars* saga has by and large already been discovered, and most aliens have already chosen sides in the long-running conflict. Some aliens are aligned with the evil Galactic Empire, some with the righteous Rebel Alliance.

Among the friendly aliens are Chewbacca, a towering member of the Wookie race who is covered in fur and enunciates his feelings in unintelligible growls and whines; Yoda, the diminutive yet wise master who trains Jedi knights, the mystic cult of heroes that dominates the saga; Jar Jar Binks, a bumbling, lizard-like creature from the planet Naboo whose role in the saga is mostly to provide comic relief; and Aayla Secura, the tentacled, blue-skinned yet sexy warrior from the Twi'lek race.

On the evil side, *Star Wars* fans have witnessed the misdeeds of such characters as Jabba the Hutt, a grumpy and obese toad-like crime boss; General Grievous, part-robot, part-living organism who is an assassin of Jedis; and the red-skinned, devil-headed Darth Maul, another assassin of Jedi knights.

The spectacular debut of Star Wars *in 1977 launched a long-running series of enormously popular films set in alien worlds. Pictured here in a scene from the 1980 movie* Star Wars Episode V: The Empire Strikes Back *is Yoda, teacher and mentor of the Jedi knights.*

Celebrating *Star Wars*

Star Wars fans remain as devoted to the series as their counterparts in the Trekkers' universe are devoted to *Star Trek*. For example, several times a year Tampa Bay, Florida, middle school teacher Jason Rucci dons an armored white uniform and helmet to attend meetings of the Tampa Bay Squad of the Florida Garrison of the 501st Legion. Anybody who has seen a movie in the *Star Wars* series will recognize the costume: Garrison members dress as the Imperial Stormtroopers, who carry out the evil orders of Lord Darth Vader and other sinister characters.

"I've gotten past people thinking we're nerds in all this,"[37] says Rucci. In fact, there are more than 40 members in the Tampa Bay Squad as well as some 250 in the Florida Garrison. Nationally, the 501st Legion includes a membership of nearly 5,000 Stormtroopers.

As for the tens of thousands of other *Star Wars* fans, many attend the annual conventions known as Star Wars Celebrations, where they dress as characters in the series, buy merchandise from vendors, sit through lectures on *Star Wars* lore, and wait in long lines for autographs from the film's stars. In 2010 the Star Wars Celebration in Tampa Bay, Florida, was attended by George Lucas, director of the first film and originator of the series. He was interviewed onstage by Comedy Central comedian and talk show host Jon Stewart, an avowed *Star Wars* fanatic. Says Rucci, "Having a cool guy like Jon Stewart admit that he is a major *Star Wars* fan takes away some of the geek factor."[38]

> ### DID YOU KNOW?
>
> One feature of the 2010 Star Wars Celebration held in Tampa Bay, Florida, was a wedding chapel in which couples could marry in front of friends dressed as aliens and Imperial Stormtroopers.

From Costumed Aliens to CGI

When the original *Star Wars* film premiered, most of the aliens were created out of latex and fabric—in other words, they were portrayed

Why Can't Spaceships Travel Faster than Light?

In many science-fiction stories, spaceships achieve interstellar travel by moving faster than the speed of light. While such a concept makes it easier for writers and filmmakers to concoct stories about alien encounters, physicists know that, in reality, faster-than-light travel is impossible.

In fact, the impossibility of traveling faster than the speed of light was first explained by mathematician Albert Einstein more than a century ago with the publication of the theory of special relativity. Special relativity states that objects gain mass as they travel faster. To maintain a faster speed, the object requires more energy. As the object approaches the speed of light, its mass would be almost infinite, and so would the energy required to maintain its speed.

"To power a rocket by propulsion . . . at something like three-quarters the speed of light for a . . . voyage to the nearest star would require an energy release that could fulfill the entire current power needs in the United States for more than 100,000 years," says Arizona State University physicist Lawrence Krauss. "This is dwarfed by the power that would be required to actually warp space."

Lawrence Krauss, *The Physics of Star Trek*. New York: Basic Books, 2007, p. 166.

by actors wearing costumes. As the series moved into the twenty-first century, computer animators took over, and now many of the *Star Wars* aliens, such as Jar Jar Binks, are created through the process of computer-generated imagery, or CGI.

In 2009 director James Cameron took CGI to its greatest heights to date by creating the aliens for the film *Avatar*. For the film, all the aliens, including the members of the race known as the Na'vi, were created by the techniques of motion capture and CGI. Moreover, the film was released in a 3-D version, truly adding a dimension to the *Avatar* aliens that other movies have lacked.

In motion capture, the actors wear costumes containing hundreds of reflective sensors, mostly sewn into the joints but appearing elsewhere

A recent addition to the alien pop culture movie universe is Avatar, *a 2009 film that explores the interaction between greedy humans and an alien civilization known as the Na'vi. The groundbreaking special effects and 3-D version of the film brought wide acclaim.*

on the costume as well. As the actors move, the camera reads the lights reflected by the sensors, making digital recordings of the actors' motions. Computers are then employed to enhance and animate the characters. For *Avatar*, motion capture and CGI techniques turned the human actors portraying the Na'vi into 10-foot-tall (3m), blue-skinned aliens whose bodies, minds, and spirits are intertwined with the natural energy of their home on the distant world of Pandora.

The story unfolds in the twenty-second century as a mining company from Earth arrives on Pandora in search of a valuable ore known as unobtanium. The miners are accompanied by a scientific team seeking to study the Na'vi; to mingle with the aliens, the scientists have created hybrid beings, or avatars, that are controlled through a psychic link to their human versions. As the avatars of the scientific team grow closer to the Na'vi and gain their trust, the mining company decides to call in the military to wipe out the Na'vi so that it can obtain the ore from Pandora.

Much of the film explores the alien civilization of the Na'vi. The Na'vi beings live among the flora and fauna of Pandora, dedicating themselves to the protection of all living things in their world. Moreover, the Na'vi are able to form psychic connections with other Pandoran creatures, as evidenced by their command of the banshees—the fierce, dinosaur-like flying beasts that are tamed under Na'vi control. As a rite of passage, each Na'vi must form a bond with a banshee. That bond enables the Na'vi to ride atop the back of the beast as it soars through the skies above the jungle world.

> **DID YOU KNOW?**
>
> By 2010 *Avatar* had sold more tickets than any movie in history, with worldwide box-office sales of more than $2.7 billion.

Environmental Messages

The story of *Avatar* may unfold on the distant world of Pandora, but its message can be found much closer to home. Clearly, the movie contains a strong environmental theme: The ruthless mining company, with the backing of an armed force, seeks to exploit the resources of an Eden-like world where creatures live in harmony with nature. The miners are so relentless in their pursuit of unobtanium that they are willing to wipe out an entire race of beings to obtain the ore.

On Earth, energy companies have often been accused of exploiting natural resources. In the meantime, as consumers burn fossil fuels, they have initiated the greenhouse effect, which is responsible for warming the planet's surface and potentially creating floods, famines, and other dire consequences. *Avatar* director Cameron says the environmental messages contained in the film are important and intentional. "Good science fiction plays as a metaphor for our current world,"[39] he says.

In *Star Trek* as well as *Avatar* and the *Star Wars* films, the story creators bent the rules of science—giving people from Earth the ability to travel great distances across the gulf of space. But when they arrive on distant planets, travelers from Earth have often found beings and cultures that are not terribly different from what they left behind. Many display human emotions and other qualities, many are steadfastly devoted to just causes, and many will fiercely defend the environments of their home planets against space travelers who have not done a very good job of protecting the ecology of their own world.

CHAPTER FIVE

Aliens Among Us

John Smith has attempted to make a new life for himself. He tries to fit in, but as with most teenagers, he often finds himself restless and uneasy. Unlike most young people, though, John harbors a deep secret—in reality he is an alien from the planet Lorien.

Nearly all the inhabitants of his planet have been wiped out. John and eight other young Loriens escaped from the cataclysmic events on their planet, which were initiated by the enemies of the Lorien race, the Modagorians. "I am told the ground shook, that the skies were full of light and explosions,"[40] John recalls in the opening pages of the 2010 novel *I Am Number Four*.

At first, John and his Lorien guardian, Henri, find a home in Arizona, but when they suspect the Modagorians have discovered them, the pair move quickly, finding a new home in Colorado. Again, John believes he has settled into a new life, but when they suspect the Modagorians are again on their trail, the pair is forced to go back on the run.

Before leaving Lorien, each of the young refugees was given a number. It was a way to protect them because the Modagorians can only kill them in order. As the title of the book indicates, as he left Lorien, John was assigned the number four. When John learns that the first three Loriens have been killed, he realizes he will be the next victim.

More than a Look Around

In many stories about extraterrestrials, the aliens simply visit Earth—they arrive, more or less, for a brief look around. Over the years, some stories about extraterrestrials have speculated on the likelihood that after arriving on the planet they decide to stay, assimilating into Earth's culture. In John Smith's case the assimilation has not been easy. Whenever he makes friends and finds a comfort level in school, he soon realizes it is time to leave and find a new hiding place.

The novel, which has been adapted into a film version with a scheduled 2011 release date, follows John as he settles in a small town in Ohio, where he decides the running must end. John, who has developed special powers such as telekinesis—the ability to move physical objects with his mind—decides to make a stand with the help of the friends he makes in his new home. Says a book critic for *Ebony* magazine, "The adventure novel takes place in a little bitty Ohio town. And, of course, there's a battle to end all battles. This is a good—no, a great—read."[41]

Aliens, Illegal and Otherwise

In *I Am Number Four*, John's main concern is fear of discovery—not by the authorities on Earth, but by his enemies, the Modagorians. Other extraterrestrial visitors have been more concerned about what would happen if the government finds them—and so they try to hide. Their plights are not unlike those of real illegal aliens who sneak across the US-Mexico border and try to assimilate into the culture of America—all the time looking over their shoulders for agents from US Immigration and Customs Enforcement.

In fact, in the opening scenes of the 1997 film *Men in Black*, border patrol agents stop a truck just after it crosses into Arizona, carrying a cargo of illegal aliens. As the customs officers order the illegal aliens to get out of the truck, a squad of mysterious government agents, all wearing black suits and dark sunglasses, show up and announce they are taking over the investigation. Their interest soon focuses on one particular alien, an old Mexican man swaddled in a blanket. As the audience soon learns, the immigrant is an extraterrestrial in disguise and in reality a snarling, lizard-like creature.

The film is based on a series of graphic novels written by Lowell Cunningham and illustrated by Sandy Carruthers, first published in 1990. The agents work for a secret government agency, MiB (the initials stand for "men in black"), responsible for keeping track of extraterrestrials on Earth. "At any one time, there are about 1,500 aliens on Earth, most of them in New York City,"[42] explains veteran Agent K to rookie Agent J. As J soon learns, most aliens do a very good job of disguising themselves as humans, but an experienced MiB agent learns to notice the stray tentacle slipping out from beneath the flap of a raincoat or the bulge made by folded antennae hidden beneath a hairpiece.

Men in Black and its 2002 sequel, *Men in Black II*, show scenes of alien visitors in many shapes, sizes, and colors, waiting at an immigration desk at MiB headquarters, papers in hand, seeking permission to enter the country. That image is similar to real-life scenes that occur every day in airports and other legal points of entry as visitors from other countries arrive in America legally. Just as it is the job of US immigration agents to track down aliens entering the country illegally, it is the job of MiB agents to seek out and arrest extraterrestrials who do not have legal authority to land on Earth.

The extraterrestrials who are allowed to enter learn to assimilate into Earth's culture, finding jobs among the residents of New York and other cities. And it is revealed in the *Men in Black* stories that many of the visitors do establish productive lives on the planet, some even gaining fame. The late Michael Jackson, one of the most eccentric singers to have achieved stardom, is revealed as an extraterrestrial. Other visitors from space unmasked by MiB include politician Newt Gingrich, former basketball star Dennis Rodman, and actor Sylvester Stallone. Says *New*

> ## DID YOU KNOW?
>
> According to Pittacus Lore, extraterrestrial author of *I Am Number Four*, aliens are responsible for creating the Loch Ness monster, lost city of Atlantis, crop circles, the Bermuda Triangle, and other mysteries of Earth.

The specter of extraterrestrials living on Earth, blending mostly unseen into daily life, was raised in the 1997 comedy Men in Black *and again in the 2002 sequel* Men in Black II. *Some of the many varieties of extraterrestrials appear in this scene from the 2002 movie.*

York Times film critic Janet Maslin, "The droll conceit of [*Men in Black*] is that this is nothing special or even strange. Perfectly unflappable, never surprised by the stray eye stalk or tentacle, the Men in Black simply go about their world-weary business."[43]

Alien Life-Forms Adapt to Earth

Men in Black and *Men in Black II* have their serious sides—in both films, MiB agents hunt down invaders with malevolent and Earth-threatening intentions. But the two films are also played for laughs. In the sequel, Agent J tracks down his retired partner, who is working at a post office in Maine. K has had his memory wiped clean and does not recall his years of service as an MiB agent. J helps bring the retired agent back to reality by quickly unmasking all the other post office workers as extraterrestrials.

Other writers as well as TV and film executives have long exploited the comic potential of extraterrestrials living among ordinary people on Earth, starting as early as 1955 with the production of a TV play titled *Visit to a Small Planet*. (It was later expanded into a Broadway play and, in 1960, a film adaptation.) The story follows a visitor to Earth who befriends a suburban family and falls in love with the family's daughter. On the visitor's home planet, affection has been outlawed. The visitor appeals to the elders at home to permit him to feel affection for the people on Earth. They agree, but after embracing the emotion of love, the visitor finds he must also accept the less desirable human emotions of hate and jealousy.

In 1963 the TV series *My Favorite Martian* premiered on American TV. The popular series (adapted into a 1999 film) followed the exploits of a Martian visitor who finds himself stranded on Earth. Moving in with a young bachelor, the Martian—known as Uncle Martin—usually succeeds in complicating life for his new roommate. That scenario was repeated with the 1978 premiere of the series *Mork & Mindy*, and again in the 1980s with the debut of the comedy series *Alf.* (Alf stood for "alien life-form.") In the TV series, Alf is a wisecracking, fur-covered runt. TV producers adapted the concept once again in the 1990s with the comedy *3rd Rock from the Sun*, which followed the antics of an interplanetary family trying to settle into life on Earth. Most recently, the concept of extraterrestrial outsiders trying hard to fit in to terrestrial life was explored in series such as *The Journey of Allen Strange*, which aired on the Nickelodeon channel from 1997 to 2000, and the Disney's Channel's 2000 made-for-TV movie *Stepsister from Planet Weird*.

Audiences could find a common theme in these comedies: They all hinged on the reactions of the visitors to the curious and often weird norms of modern American culture. On *Mork & Mindy*, for example, the space visitor Mork, played by Robin Williams at the beginning of his career in comedy, would constantly misinterpret the messages conveyed to him on Earth. For example, when a doctor advises Mork that he needs more iron in his diet, Mork wonders out loud whether he should eat his car keys. And when Mork sees a young man and young woman arguing, he wonders whether that type of conduct is natural. His friend Mindy advises Mork that it is very natural, and in fact the two young people are probably in love. Well, Mork says, from what he has seen in the movies, the cowboys and Indians must have really been in love.

Mip! The Coneheads

Even more unusual interpretations of Earth culture could be found in the Coneheads segments of *Saturday Night Live* (and in a 1993 film adaptation of the long-running parody). The Coneheads—husband Beldar, wife Prymaat, and teenage daughter Connie—have immigrated to Earth from the planet Remulak. By all accounts, they are an ordinary suburban

> **DID YOU KNOW?**
>
> Among *Alf*'s biggest fans were President Ronald Reagan and First Lady Nancy Reagan. The Reagans admitted they never missed an episode.

Aliens Walk Among Us at Comic-Con

Science-fiction fans who attended the 2010 Comic-Con International event in San Diego, California, were greeted by about a half dozen Men in Black "agents" distributing flyers publicizing the third film in the series, which has an expected release date of 2012. Elsewhere at the convention, which is attended by some 125,000 people a year, visitors could find fans dressed as extraterrestrials from such films and TV shows as *Predator, Star Wars, Battlestar Galactica,* and *Alien.*

Comic-Con International was founded in 1970 by comic book fan Sheldon Dorf to give readers an opportunity to mingle with the artists, writers, and publishers who create characters such as Superman, Spider-Man, and the Incredible Hulk. The event has since grown beyond the comic book world, encompassing films, graphic novels, TV shows, and other elements of popular culture.

It is not unusual for fans who attend the four-day event at the San Diego Convention Center to dress as their favorite characters, which often include assorted extraterrestrials. "It's a zoo. It's a Halloween zoo," said actor Ben Foster while attending Comic-Con to publicize his 2009 science-fiction film *Pandorum.* "I have no idea how to process this place. It's funny . . . I'm not accustomed to seeing this many people dressed up in samurai outfits and aliens, all in one space."

Quoted in Sandy Cohen, Associated Press, "Strange, Scary, Wondrous," *Arlington Heights (IL) Daily Herald,* July 26, 2009, p. 20.

family (Beldar owns a driving school), but they do share one obvious feature that sets them apart from their neighbors: Their heads are in the shape of cones. Still, they have established comfortable lives as they try to assimilate into American society.

There are occasional moments when the Coneheads are puzzled by life on Earth. When Connie arrives home from school and announces she is planning to attend a rock concert, Beldar admits that he does not understand young people's music. "Mip!" Beldar complains, "I cannot

The popular television comedy show Saturday Night Live *introduced its own brand of Earth-dwelling aliens with the family known as the Coneheads (pictured). The Coneheads continuously tried, usually with humorous results, to assimilate into American culture.*

comprehend those irregular sound patterns that you enjoy."[44] And when Connie says she is bored with school and wants to return home to Remulak, Beldar explodes in a rage: "Hear me, young one: you are privileged. When I was a small cone, my family lived in an isolated quadron. I had to walk ten dextrons, knee-deep in farlite-crystals each day, to a little red one-room data center!"[45] Occasionally, the Coneheads draw curious stares and uncomfortable questions from humans. Beldar always has a quick response to their inquiries, though, particularly when it comes to identifying their homeland. He always tells people his family comes from France.

No Language Barriers

Another common thread that connects the stories behind Uncle Martin, Mork, Alf, and even John Smith and the *Men in Black* aliens is that no matter what planet they may call home, they all manage to speak English once they arrive on Earth. Indeed, while it is likely that aliens have their own languages on their home planets, Carl Sagan believed there could be an actual scientific reason for why aliens are so fluent in English (and the other native languages of Earth).

According to Sagan, alien civilizations have been spending the last several decades watching TV shows produced on Earth. Those signals are broadcast into space, where they are intercepted by satellites and redirected back to TV sets on Earth. However, the signals also go well past the satellites orbiting the planet, traveling at the speed of light, where they are eventually intercepted by TV receivers on distant planets. Said Sagan,

> **DID YOU KNOW?**
>
> William Shatner is best known for his role as Captain James Kirk, discoverer of many alien life-forms, but in the TV comedy *3rd Rock from the Sun,* Shatner played an alien known as the Big Giant Head.

> The most frequently repeated messages will be station call signals and appeals to purchase detergents, deodorants, headache tablets and automobile and petroleum products. . . . The mindless contents of commercial television and [news] of international crisis and warfare within the human family are the principal messages about life on Earth that we choose to broadcast to the cosmos. What must they think of us?[46]

Accepting Them for Who They Are

Unlike the Coneheads or the aliens from the *Men in Black* films, some extraterrestrials have decided to be very open about who they are. They want to assimilate into Earth society, to be sure, but they do not want

Who Is Pittacus Lore?

The author of *I Am Number Four* and additional novels planned as sequels is listed on the book's cover as Pittacus Lore. According to the series' website, Pittacus Lore is an elder from the planet Lorien. He or she (the website does not identify the author's gender) is 10,000 years old and has taken on the responsibility of recounting the saga of the Loriens and the nine young people who escaped the war against the Modagorians. Says the author:

> I am telling the story of Lorien, the Nine, and the war at hand so you do not allow the same thing that happened to us happen to you. I am trying to find the Nine and unite them. They may be walking past you right now, or sitting near you, or watching you as you read this. They may be in your city, your town. If they are doing what they are supposed to be doing, they are living anonymously, training, and waiting for the day when they will find each other, and me, and we will make our last stand together.

Pittacus Lore, "To the People of Earth," 2010. http://iamnumberfourfans.com/pittacus-lore.

to lose their identities as extraterrestrials. As with most immigrants, they hope people will accept them for who they are.

That scenario was the basis for the 1988 film, *Alien Nation*, which also spawned several novels and a TV series. The story centers on the lives of Newcomers, aliens from the planet Tencton who have immigrated to Earth. (According to the story, more than 250,000 have moved into the city of Los Angeles.) They make no attempts to disguise themselves; although humanoid, the Newcomers can be recognized by their bald, spotted and slightly oversized heads.

Many of the Newcomers have done a very good job of assimilating into Earth culture, although—like many immigrants—the Newcomers often face discrimination and abuse. On Earth, a derogatory term for a Newcomer is "slag." Some have turned to crime, which is why the Los Angeles Police Department has found it necessary to recruit Newcomers for the detective force. *Alien Nation* follows the adventures of one New-comer, Sam Francisco, as he teams up with detective Matthew Sykes to solve a series of murders.

At first, the hard-boiled Sykes is loathe to accept the sensitive and cerebral Francisco as his partner, but eventually the Newcomer earns his partner's trust, and together they chase down the culprits. Science-fiction writer and literary critic Thomas M. Disch says *Alien Nation* reflects the true immigrant experience in America in that the Newcomers are new to the country, they have a different look than their neighbors, and their tastes in clothes, music, and food often reflect their heritages rather than their new environments. "Aliens are people very much like us, entitled to have their fair share of the American pie," says Disch. "There are some multicultural differences, of course: the Newcomers have some peculiar food preferences . . . and their taste in home furnishings can seem garish. But they have adapted to their new home."[47]

> **DID YOU KNOW?**
>
> In the 2008 film *Meet Dave*, aliens arrive on Earth inside a spacecraft in the shape of a human being.

Wide-Eyed Amazement

As the plight of the Newcomers illustrates, some extraterrestrials arrive on Earth as friends, some as lawbreakers. That has been the case since aliens first burst into popular culture more than a century ago with the publication of *The War of the Worlds*. Certainly, the aliens of H.G. Wells's novel were by no means on friendly terms with anyone they found on Earth, but other aliens have shown they can live on Earth in peace. Whether Klaatu was concerned with nuclear proliferation, as he was in 1951, or with environmental destruction, as he was in 2008, the visitor from another planet showed compassion for the people of Earth.

Other aliens, such as Mork and Beldar, have displayed wide-eyed amazement at what they have discovered about their new homes. And since the earliest days of science-fiction literature and films, it has been clear that humans have also expressed a wide-eyed amazement about extraterrestrials and the stories they can tell.

SOURCE NOTES

Introduction: The Enduring Popularity of Extraterrestrials

1. H.G. Wells, *The War of the Worlds*. Clayton, DE: Prestwick House, 2006, pp. 11–12.
2. Wells, *The War of the Worlds*, p. 158.
3. John Clute, *The Illustrated Encyclopedia of Science Fiction*. London: Dorling Kindersley, 1995, p. 23.
4. Quoted in Stuart Elliott, "Alien Advertising Has Landed, Earthlings, and It Is Taking Over," *New York Times*, July 2, 1997, p. D-5.
5. Sidney Perkowitz, *Hollywood Science: Movies, Science, and the End of the World*. New York: Columbia University Press, 2007, p. 19.
6. Quoted in Hana Baba, "Senior Astronomer Seth Shostak on the Search for Extraterrestrial Intelligence," *San Francisco Chronicle*, August 12, 2010. www.sfgate.com.
7. Quoted in *New York Times*, "Radio Listeners in Panic, Taking War Drama as Fact," October 31, 1938; reprint. www.war-of-the-worlds.org.
8. Stephen King, *Danse Macabre*. New York: Berkley, 1983, p. 117.

Chapter One: The Aliens Arrive

9. Quoted in Bayla Singer, *Like Sex with Gods: An Unorthodox History of Flying*. College Station: Texas A&M University Press, 2003, p. 72.
10. Camille Flammarion, *Uranie*. New York: Cassell, 1899, p. 36.
11. Clute, *The Illustrated Encyclopedia of Science Fiction*, p. 90.
12. Percival Lowell, *Mars and Its Canals*. New York: MacMillan, 1906, p. 382.
13. Carl Sagan, *Cosmos*. New York: Random House, 1980, p. 110.
14. *Baltimore Sun*, "The War of the Worlds," March 28, 1898, p. 10.

Chapter Two: They Come to Conquer

15. Charles Taylor, "Invasion of the Student Body Snatchers," Salon. com, January 15, 1999. www.salon.com.

16. Quoted in Bruce Rux, *Hollywood vs. the Aliens: The Motion Picture Industry's Participation in UFO Disinformation*. Berkeley, CA: Frog, 1997, p. 105.

17. Rux, *Hollywood vs. the Aliens*, p. 109.

18. Quoted in J.P. Telotte, *The Science Fiction Film*. Cambridge: Cambridge University Press, 2001, p. 181.

19. King, *Danse Macabre*, p. 149.

20. Quoted in Lynn Spigel and Michael Curtin, eds., *The Revolution Wasn't Televised*. New York: Routledge, 1997, p. 21.

21. Quoted in Rux, *Hollywood vs. the Aliens*, p. 326.

22. Quoted in Diane Toroian, "X-Philes Gather Here for Two-Day 'Relaxacon,'" *St. Louis Post-Dispatch*, November 20, 1997, p. G-1.

23. Quoted in Dean A. Kowalski and William B. Davis, eds., *The Philosophy of the X-Files*. Lexington: University Press of Kentucky, 2007, p. 19.

24. Quoted in Lewis Wallace, "*Battle: Los Angeles* Mixes UFO Lore, Fallujah Feel," *UFO Digest*, July 25, 2010. www.ufodigest.com.

Chapter Three: They Come in Peace

25. Quoted in Clark Collis, "Comic-Con Preview," *Entertainment Weekly*, July 23, 2010, p. 42.

26. Clute, *The Illustrated Encyclopedia of Science Fiction*, p. 262.

27. Quoted in Kristen Lewis, "*The Day the Earth Stood Still*," *Scholastic Scope*, March 23, 2009, p. 10.

28. Quoted in Steve Biodrowski, "*The Day the Earth Stood Still*—Preview," *Cinefantastique*, December 6, 2008. http://cinefantastiqueon line.com.

29. *Outer Limits*, "Trial by Fire," Yahoo TV, March 3, 1996. http://tv.yahoo.com.

30. Quoted in Ray Morton, *Close Encounters of the Third Kind: The Making of Steven Spielberg's Classic Film*. New York: Applause, 2007, p. 288.

31. Rux, *Hollywood vs. the Aliens*, pp. 512–13.

32. Les Daniels, *Superman: The Complete History—the Life and Times of the Man of Steel*. San Francisco: Chronicle, 2004, p. 19.

Chapter Four: Off-World Encounters

33. William Shatner, *Up Till Now: The Autobiography*. New York: Thomas Dunne, 2008, pp. 121–22.

34. John Tulloch and Henry Jenkins, *Science Fiction Audiences: Watching Doctor Who and Star Trek*. New York: Routledge, 1995, p. 4.

35. Richard Zoglin, "Trekking Onward," *Time*, November 28, 1994, p. 72.

36. Quoted in Denny Angelle, "Star Trek Mania," *Boys' Life*, July 1992, p. 22.

37. Quoted in Walt Belcher, "Orlando Hosts Tour de Force," *Tampa Tribune*, August 10, 2010, p. 8.

38. Quoted in Belcher, "Orlando Hosts Tour de Force," p. 8.

39. Quoted in Michael Cieply, "On Screens Soon, Abused Earth Gets Its Revenge," *New York Times*, March 12, 2007, p. 1.

Chapter Five: Aliens Among Us

40. Pittacus Lore, *I Am Number Four*. New York: HarperCollins, 2010, p. 5.

41. *Ebony*, "*I Am Number Four*," October 2010, p. 43.

42. Quoted in Brian D. Johnson, "A Frolic in the Alien Fun House," *Maclean's*, July 14, 1997, p. 62.

43. Janet Maslin, "Oh, Aliens: Business as Usual," *New York Times*, July 1, 1997, p. C-9.

44. *Saturday Night Live* Transcripts, "The Coneheads at Home," February 26, 1977. http://snltranscripts.jt.org.

45. *Saturday Night Live* Transcripts, "The Coneheads at Home."

46. Sagan, *Cosmos*, p. 286.

47. Thomas M. Disch, *The Dreams Our Stuff Is Made Of: How Science Fiction Conquered the World*. New York: Free Press, 1998, p. 189.

Books

Terry J. Erdmann and Paula M. Block, *Star Trek 101*. New York: Pocket, 2008.

Jack Hagerty and Jon Rogers, *The Saucer Fleet*. Burlington, ON: Apogee, 2008.

Dean A. Kowalski and William B. Davis, eds., *The Philosophy of the X-Files*. Lexington: University Press of Kentucky, 2007.

Lawrence Krauss, *The Physics of Star Trek*. New York: Basic Books, 2007.

Ray Morton, *Close Encounters of the Third Kind: The Making of Steven Spielberg's Classic Film*. New York: Applause, 2007.

Sidney Perkowitz, *Hollywood Science: Movies, Science, and the End of the World*. New York: Columbia University Press, 2007.

J.W. Rinzler, *The Making of Star Wars*. New York: Ballantine, 2007.

Maria Wilhelm and Dirk Mathison, *Avatar: An Activist Survivor Guide*. New York: HarperCollins, 2009.

Websites

Hugo Awards (www.thehugoawards.org). Sponsored by the World Science Fiction Society, the awards are presented each year to the best books and stories written in the science-fiction genre. Visitors to the organization's website can find lists of Hugo Award winners dating back to 1953. The awards are named in honor of Hugo Gernsback, the first publisher of *Amazing Stories* magazine.

J. Allen Hynek Center for UFO Studies (www.cufos.org). Founded by the late Northwestern University astronomer who coined the phrase "close encounters of the third kind," visitors to the organization's website can find many resources about UFO sightings and extraterrestrials, including government documents, eyewitness accounts, and articles published in the center's newsletter, the *International UFO Reporter.*

Star Wars Celebration (www.starwarscelebration.com). Official website of Star Wars Celebration, the annual event in which fans can trade rumors and trivia about developments in the *Star Wars* universe, meet the creative people involved in the films, and dress up as their favorite aliens. The site includes news about the annual event as well as ticket availability and hotel accommodations.

"Top 30 Alien Invasion Movies," *Boston Globe* (www.boston.com/ae/movies/gallery/topinvasionmovies). Sponsored by the *Boston Globe*, the newspaper's film critics provide a ranking of the top 30 films in the alien invasion genre, including a synopsis and photo from each movie on the list.

The War of the Worlds, **Sacred Texts** (www.sacred-texts.com/ufo/mars/wow.htm). The script for the hour-long radio adaptation of *The War of the Worlds* that aired October 30, 1938, can be read at this website. The producers altered the story, presenting it as a newscast. Despite announcements that the story was fictional, the broadcast caused widespread panic among people who believed Earth was under Martian attack.

INDEX

Note: Boldface page numbers indicate illustrations.

Aayla Secura (*Star Wars*), 55
Action Comics, 39
advertisements, 6
Aelita: Queen of Mars (1924 film), 22
Airship, The (1917 film), 20, 22
Alf (television series), 66
Alien Nation (1988 film), 70–71
All-Story (magazine), 15–16
Amazing Stories (magazine), 11, 15, 16
Anderson, Gillian, 33
Andorians *(Star Trek),* 50
Anthea, 39–40
Apollo moon missions, 48
Area 51, 36
Arnold, Kenneth, 27
astronomy, 12, 13
Atari, *Space Invaders* (video game), 28
Avatar (2009 film)
    creation of aliens in, 57–58
    popularity of, 59
    theme of, 59–60

banshees, 59
Battle: Los Angeles (2011 film), 35
Behind the Flying Saucers (Scully), 24
Berg, Jon, 54
Bergerac, Cyrano de, 10
books
    Behind the Flying Saucers (Scully), 24
    First Men in the Moon (Wells), 19
    Hitchhiker's Guide to the Galaxy, The (Adams), 47
    I Am Number Four (Lore), 61, 62
    Inhabitants of the Other World, The (Flammarion), 12
    Journey to the Centre of the Earth (Verne), 9
    Man Who Fell to Earth, The (Tevis), 38–40
    Micromégas (Voltaire), 10–11
    Mount, The (Emshwiller), 34
    Plurality of Inhabited Worlds, The (Flammarion), 12

Star (Defontenay), 11–12
Superman: The Dark Side (DC Comics), 45
Time Machine, The (Wells), 9
Twenty Thousand Leagues Under the Sea (Verne), 9
War of the Worlds, The (Wells), 4–5, **5**, 6, 7, **14**, 15
Yellow Blue Tibia (Roberts), 34
Burroughs, Edgar Rice, 15–16

Cage, Nicholas, 38
Cameron, James, 57, 59–60
Carruthers, Sandy, 63
Center for UFO studies, 44
Chewbacca *(Star Wars),* 55
Clive *(Paul),* 36
close encounters, defined, 40, 42
Close Encounters of the Third Kind (1977 film), 40, **41**, 42, 44
Clute, John, 6, 37
Comical History of the States and Empires of the Moon (de Bergerac), 10
comic books/strips
    Comic-Con International, 67
    Flash Gordon, 16, **17**, 18
    Superman, 39, 45, 46
Comic-Con International, 67
communism
    films and, 22, 24–26, **25**
    television and, 53
computer-generated imagery (CGI), 57, 58
Coneheads (Saturday Night Live), 66–68, **68**
Crabbe, Buster, 18
Cruise, Tom, 5–6
Cunningham, Lowell, 63

Dana Scully *(The X-Files),* 30–31
Daniels, Les, 46–47
Darkest Hour, The (2011 film), 35
Darth Maul, 55
Darwin, Charles, 12–13
Day the Earth Stood Still, The (1951 film), 37
Day the Earth Stood Still, The (2008 film), 38

Defontenay, Charlemagne-Ischir, 11–12
Denby, David, 34
Derrickson, Scott, 38
Disch, Thomas M., 71
dolphins, 47
Dorf, Sheldon, 67
Dr. Who (television series), 28, 34
Duchovny, David, 33

Ebony (magazine), 62
Einstein, Albert, 57
Elliott *(E.T.: The Extraterrestrial),* 44–45
Emshwiller, Carol, 34
English language, 69
Enterprise, 49, 52–53
environment and films, 38–40, 59–60
E.T.: The Extraterrestrial (1982 film), 42–45, **43**
evolution, 12–13

Faculty, The (1998 film), 23–24
Fanning, Dakota, 5–6
films
    Aelita: Queen of Mars, 22
    Airship, The (Himmelskibet), 20, 22
    Alien Nation, 70–71
    Avatar, 57–60
    Battle: Los Angeles, 35
    Clone Wars, The, 54
    Close Encounters of the Third Kind, 40, **41**, 42, 44
    communism and, 22, 24–26, **25**
    Darkest Hour, The, 35
    Day the Earth Stood Still, The (1951), 37
    Day the Earth Stood Still, The (2008), 38
    early, 19–20, **21**, 22
    environment and, 38–40
    E.T.: The Extraterrestrial, 42–45, **43**
    Faculty, The, 23–24
    Flash Gordon, 18, 20
    Halo, 35
    Independence Day, 30

PICTURE CREDITS

ABOUT THE AUTHOR

Hal Marcovitz is a former newspaper reporter and columnist and the author of more than 150 books for young readers. He makes his home in Chalfont, Pennsylvania.